THE ISRAEL of GOD

Sorting Out the Confusion between Historical Israel, Spiritual Israel, and the Current Nation of Israel

Vic Reasoner

3080 Brannon Rd
Nicholasville, KY 40356-9700

ISBN 979-8-9957589-1-4
Library of Congress Control Number:
2026943554

TABLE of CONTENTS

Definition of Terms 4
Classic Methodist Interpretation 8
Representative Methodist Exegesis 13
Help from the Book of Hebrews 27
Covenant Theology 31
False Conclusions Based on False Interpretations 35
Conclusion 47
Bibliography 48

THE ISRAEL of GOD

When I was nineteen I was trying to preach at City Union Mission in Kansas City. Someone interrupted me, "Preacher, I just have one question — was Jesus a Jew?" Like a flash other men in the congregation began to hiss and I thought a riot was going to break out. Security stepped in before I had a chance to say anything. However, I don't think I was prepared to say anything beyond, "yes, certainly Jesus was Jewish." Apparently I had encountered a stronghold of antisemitism.

Now, over a half-century later, my conclusion is that the Jew is no better nor any worse than the rest of the human race. He or she will be saved by grace through faith in Jesus Christ, just like every other sinner.

We must unravel Israel historically, Israel spiritually, and Israel politically. The conservative political movement today is divided over hatred for Jews or whether Christians are obligated to support the nation of Israel unconditionally. I reject both extremes.

Definition of terms

Israel is the name given to Jacob when he wrestled with God (Gen 32:28). How did this personal name become a national identity? While *Jacob* meant crooked, God is straight. Within the wordplay, *Israel* describes the one whom God has straightened out. And so Israel is one who is straight or right with God by keeping God's covenant.

Jew is derived from Jacob's fourth son, Judah. More broadly *Jew* means one who rejects idolatry and worships the one true God. When the northern kingdom did not return from captivity, the term *Jew* was expanded to include all Israelites regardless of which tribe. When Jerusalem fell in AD 70 genealogical records were lost and today no one knows for sure which tribe they belong to. In general Judaism is passed on through the mother's blood line. Yet neither Ishmael nor Esau were identified as Jews.

Today Jewish identity is confirmed religiously, as defined by rabbinic law, legally and politically, as defined by Israeli law, or culturally/ethnically, as defined by self-identification. None of these criteria match Paul's definition.

According to Romans 2:28-29 a Jew has been redefined to include all believers. Mark Hanna wrote, "Israel today is not the people of God." He argued that the people of God today are not Israelis or Jews or Gentiles, but regenerated believers in the gospel of Christ.[1]

It should be obvious from Romans 9:6 that the term *Israel* carries more than one meaning. Paul declared, "For not all who are descended from Israel belong to Israel." He is making a distinction between historical Israel and spiritual

---

[1]Hanna, "Israel Today," 14-17. This article in *Christianity Today* was followed by an attempted rebuttal by Jerry Falwell entitled "Jerry Falwell Objects," 14-17. In his agenda for the Moral Majority, Falwell declared, "To stand against Israel is to stand against God" [*Fundamentalist Phenomenon*, 215]. However, Falwell was advocating a political agenda. Falwell declares that the future of the State of Israel is more important than any other political question and that the Jews have a theological, historical, and legal right to Palestine [Simon, *Jerry Falwell and the Jews*, 62, 68].

Israel.

In an old commentary, written about AD 375 by an unknown author, but attributed to "Ambrosiaster," three different meanings of the name *Jew* were given. First, it meant the children of Abraham. Then it refers to Jacob and his son Judah. Third, they are called Jews, not because of Judah, but because of Christ, who was born to the tribe of Judah. The praise associated with Judah's name and his designation as "master" (Judg 20:18) have been transferred to Christ.[2]

A Greek-English Lexicon of the New Testament followed this same threefold definition for the word *Israel*, stating that in a figurative sense Christians are the true nation of Israel.[3] Since the Jews were a nation formed by covenant, not a race formed by blood, with the passing away of the old covenant, there is no longer any such thing as a Jew in the biblical sense. After AD 70 there were no longer any true Jews, except those who had become Christians.

John McClintock and James Strong defined *Israel* as the true people of God, whether of Jewish or gentile origin; comprising the entire church of the redeemed.[4] Godet said that the "many Gentiles converted to the gospel who, all uncircumcised as they were, nevertheless fulfill the law in virtue of the spirit of Christ, and thus become the *true* Israel, *the Israel of God*."[5]

Steve Gregg explained that the term *Israel* had no less than five meanings. It was used for a man's name, the descen-

---

[2]Bray, *ACCS*, 6:71.

[3]Arndt and Gingrich, *Lexicon*, 381.

[4]McClintock and Strong, *Cyclopedia*, 4:694.

[5]Godet, *Commentary*, 130.

dants of that man, the covenant nation in which those descendants formed the ethnic majority, and the defined territory controlled by the nation, and the faithful remnant who truly kept God's covenant.[6]

In Romans 4:9-12 where we are told that Abraham is the father of the faithful. William Barclay concluded, "In one short paragraph Paul has shattered all Jewish thought."[7] God does not have two people nor two plans. Both Jew and Gentile are to be incorporated into "one new man." The dividing wall has been destroyed (Eph 2:14-15). If God's plan is for the new corporate man, which is the church, why does dispensationalism insist that God still retains a plan for unbelieving Israel separate from the church? Snodgrass explained, "Dispensationalists are eager to keep this text from saying Gentiles are now part of Israel."[8]

According to Peter, God put no difference between Jew and Gentile (Acts 15:9). Ray Dunning wrote, "The most pervasive metaphor used in the New Testament for the Church is 'the new Israel.'" He then rejected dispensationalism. "The distinction between Israel and the Church, so widely embraced among conservative Christians, simply will not stand the test of biblical exegesis."[9]

I am not quibbling over the terms *covenant* or *dispensation*. If a dispensation is a method of administration, the term *dispensation* could be a near synonymous term with covenant.

---

[6]Gregg, *There Is Another King*, 54.

[7]Barclay, *Romans*, 66.

[8]Snodgrass, *Ephesians*, 143.

[9]Dunning, *Grace, Faith, and Holiness*, 511-512. It should be clarified however that not all "conservative" Christians are dispensational.

The real distinction is that covenant theology sees continuity, while dispensationalism teaches a split covenant between Israel and the church.

Classic Methodist Interpretation

In the history of interpretation, Justin Martyr, writing in the second century, condemned Judaism because Christianity had inherited all that was valuable, religiously, doctrinally, and messianically, in Judaism. Therefore, Jews need to be converted.[10] Alan Patrick Boyd surveyed the church fathers up to AD 165 and concluded, "The majority of the writers/ writings in this period completely identify Israel with the Church."[11]

Jacob Arminius taught that God's covenant with Israel was both corporate and conditional. The fact that most Jews rejected Jesus Christ does not mean that the Word of God has failed since the covenant was based on faith.[12]

If Israel was unconditionally elect, Paul would not write in Romans 11 that they were cut off. Nor would Zechariah declare in 11:10-14 that God would revoke his covenant with Israel. But their apostasy was not final because in Romans 11:26 Paul prophesies that they *will be* saved. Again, he is speaking corporately. But if the covenant with Israel was unconditional, they would have never *not* been saved.

While I am surveying classic Methodist commentaries, the position I am documenting is not unique to Methodists.

---

[10]Justin Martyr, *Dialogue with Trypho*, ch. 137; *ANF* 1:268.

[11]Boyd, "A Dispensational Premillennial Analysis of the Eschatology of the Post-Apostolic Fathers," 47.

[12]Arminius, *Works*, 3:489-495.

The transfer of conditional privilege from historic Israel to the church is a doctrine which is affirmed by both Calvinism and Wesleyan-Arminians. For example, see Oswald T. Allis, *Prophecy and the Church* (1945). The subtitle explains, "an examination of the claim of dispensationalists that the Christian church is a mystery parenthesis which interrupts the fulfilment to Israel of the kingdom prophecies of the Old Testament." While Allis represents historic Calvinism, his conclusion could have been written by a Methodist:

> The Church is not a mystery in the sense that it is an unexpected and temporary interruption of the prophetic plan for Israel. It does not interrupt: it unfolds and fulfils that program. . . . The wall of separation between Jew and Gentile has been broken down. The limitations and peculiarities of Judaism have been done away. They have been done away not for the time being only, but for ever. They are never to be restored. There is a great and glorious future for the Jew. But that future is to be found in and through the Christian Church.[13]

George Eldon Ladd, a historical, rather than a dispensational, premillennialist Baptist said,

> I do not see how it is possible to avoid the conclusion that the New Testament applies Old Testament prophecies to the New Testament church and in so doing identified the church as spiritual Israel.[14]

---

[13]Allis, *Prophecy and the Church*, 258-259.

[14]Ladd, "Historic Premillennialism," 23.

Ladd's statement could also be affirmed by Methodism. The church has historically taught that Israel was the Old Testament church and that the New Testament church was the new Israel of God.

Not until John Darby (1800-1882) was it ever claimed that the church was an interruption of God's plan with Israel. Darby taught that when Israel rejected the kingdom, the church became a parenthesis in God's plan. According to Clarence Bass the first time the Church had ever been called a parenthesis is when John Darby did so in 1830. Darby explained that the present time is called a parenthesis between Daniel's 69 weeks and the last week.[15] This view was made popular by the *Scofield Reference Bible* (1909).

The first book Daniel Steele wrote was *A Substitute for Holiness*.[16] Of particular interest is a passage in the book telling of an encounter Steele had with John Darby. Steele was especially concerned with the implications of discarding the doctrine of the general judgment. Steele asked Darby for an exposition of Matthew 25:31-46. Steele said, "We could hardly keep from laughing in the face of the venerable Christian scholar. . . . What pitiable make-shifts to explain away this most solemn and awful passage in the Holy Scriptures!" According to Darby this was not a final and universal judgment, but a review of Gentile nations. Individuals are not being judged, but nations will be judged on the basis of how they treated the Christianized Jews whom Christ will send fourth to convert the Gentiles after His coming to set up a visible kingdom on earth. Steele continued,

---

[15]Bass, *Backgrounds to Dispensationalism*, 129.

[16]However, he edited *The People's Commentary* in 1879, which was produced by his father-in-law, Amos Binney.

> But when pressed to explain more particularly the sheep and the goats, and the final sentence, the wriggling and floundering of this great evangelist was something wonderful to behold. May I never see another man, manifestly of so great genius and learning, compelled to crawl through orifices so small. There is some thing very depressing to a generous mind to witness such an intellectual humiliation in the attempt to save a baseless dogma from a manifest overthrow.[17]

It is sometimes pointed out that Adam Clarke predicted the "rebirth" of Israel as a nation. What Clarke actually said was that "the fulness of the Gentiles shall be brought in" by AD 1947. This is hailed as a remarkable prediction since it was in 1947 that the U. N. partitioned Palestine to create the state of Israel. However, Clarke did not anticipate the formation of Israel as a nation; for him bringing in the fullness of the gentiles meant their salvation and entrance into the kingdom of God which would lead to the millennium. Clarke describes this as a time when wars would cease. Jew and gentile would become one fold, and God properly worshiped over the face of the whole earth.[18] Dispensationalists, however, read into Clarke their own presuppositions. They would connect Clarke's reference to the fullness of the gentiles to Luke 21:24 which states that "Jerusalem will be trampled on by the Gentiles until the times of the Gentiles are fulfilled." For Jerusalem to once again come under Jewish control is interpreted dispensationally to mean that the church age is

---

[17]Steele, *A Substitute for Holiness*, 85.

[18]Clarke, Commentary, 4:619.

over. The close of the church age is brought about by a secret rapture and God's agenda then becomes the establishment of a Jewish kingdom. This is not what Clarke anticipated nor did this happen in 1947.[19]

In 1851 Richard Watson said that if Israel would ever be gathered again as a nation, it would be as God's ancient, not his peculiar, people. It would not be in any special covenant.[20] Of course, Israel did become a nation in 1948 but the debated issue is what theological significance, if any, did that event have. The modern political nation of Israel is a secular state with no biblical or prophetic significance.

Methodist exegesis has always understood the New Testament church as inheriting the promises made to Old Testament Israel. A survey of comments on passages Romans 2:28-29, 4:9-16; 9:6; 10:12; 11:26; Galatians 3:7, 29, 6:16; Ephesians 2:12-19; Philippians 3:3; 1 Peter 2:9; and Revelation 3:9 will reveal that Methodism has consistently followed this hermeneutic. For example, Thomas Coke wrote that since the Christian church succeeded the Jewish, it has the same titles of *elect* and *sanctified*.[21] Wesley, in his comments on Matthew 1:21 declared that Jesus came to save Israel "and all

---

[19]"Daniel Told Us! Adam Clarke Showed Us," 16-17. Ralph Earle also cited Clarke's predictions for 1947 and 1966. He asked, "How could Adam Clarke make these precise predictions 150 years ago exactly to the year, as we have now seen them fulfilled? We have no answer, unless this was what these scriptures were intended to mean." However, Earle made no reference to the other two predictions: 1902 and 2015 [*What the Bible Says About the Second Coming*, 85-87].

[20]Watson, *Sermons*, "The Shaking of Heaven and Earth," Sermon #99, 2:102.

[21]Coke, *Commentary*, 6:779.

the Israel of God."[22]

Representative Methodist Exegesis on Spiritual Israel

Romans 2:28-29

John Wesley defined a *Jew* as "one of God's beloved people."[23] Richard Watson wrote in his commentary, "He is not a true son of Abraham, a member of that spiritual Church of which the visible Church of the Jews was but the sensible form, who has nothing but natural birth and fleshly circumcision to plead."[24] Watson defined *Israel* as referring either to the person of Jacob, the whole race of Jacob, the kingdom of Israel as distinct from the kingdom of Judah, or the spiritual Israel, the true church of God.[25]

Joseph Benson explained, "The circumcision which renders men the sons of Abraham, and the people of God, *is of the heart*."[26] Clarke wrote that the Jew described in v 29 was "a true member of the Church of God."[27]

Romans 4:9-16

Abraham is not the father of the circumcised; he is the

---

[22]Wesley, *Notes*, 11.

[23]Wesley, *Notes*, 368.

[24]Watson, *Exposition*, 485.

[25]Watson, *Biblical and Theological Dictionary*, 496.

[26]Benson, *Notes*, 5:33.

[27]Clarke, *Commentary*, 6:52.

father of those who believe. Therefore, if Jews want to be included in the Abrahamic covenant, they must believe along with gentiles. "To those who believe not, Abraham is not a father, neither are they his seed," said Wesley. The promises is to all "the spiritual seed of Abraham; not only Jews, but Gentiles also, if they follow his faith."[28] Nathaniel Burwash explained that Abraham was the father "of both the legal and the spiritual seed."[29]

Adam Clarke taught that Abraham himself was a Gentile when he received God's promise. For the Jews to be saved, they must come under the Abrahamic covenant, "in which the Gentiles are included." "Both Jews and Gentiles, who, believing in Christ Jesus, have a right to all the blessings contained in the Abrahamic covenant."[30]

Benson concluded that "the justification of those who are out of the visible church, but who believe and obey God, is implied. . . . Heathen, therefore, who believe and obey the true God, as Abraham did, will, like him, have their faith counted to them for righteousness, though not members of any visible church."[31] Abraham is

> The spiritual father of all true believers; the original witness of justifying faith, after whose type, as the first public example of it, all were to be molded, whether Jew or Gentile, who should thereafter attain

---

[28]Wesley, *Notes*, 372-373. Benson made a similar statement [*Notes*, 5:44].

[29]Burwash, *Romans*, 88.

[30]Clarke, *Commentary*, 6:62-63.

[31]Benson, *Notes*, 5:43. Coke made the same point [*Commentary*, 6:41].

unto salvation.[32]

Daniel Whedon wrote that the phrase *father of us all* in v 16:

> boldly and forever inserts the Christian Church into sonship to Abraham. . . . And of this new universal Church, in which Jew and Gentile distinctions no longer exist, the ancient father still is Abraham. . . . The Old Testament Church and the New Testament Church have the same foundation. Believers in Christ are the true sons of Abraham; the true Christian is the true Jew.[33]

Thomas Coke declared:

> The whole of the Apostle's argument in this chapter proves, that we believing Gentiles are the seed of Abraham, to whom, as well as to himself, the promise was made; consequently it is the Abrahamic covenant in which we now stand, and any argument taken from the nature of that covenant, and applied to ourselves, must be good and valid. . . . But we may forfeit this birth-right, and shall certainly lose it for ever, if we prefer the pleasures of sin before the favor of God.[34]

William G. Williams concluded,

---

[32]Binney, *The People's Commentary*, 404.

[33]Whedon, *Commentary*, 3:322, 324.

[34]Coke, *Commentary*, 6:44.

> And so the text says that God made all this gracious provision expressly to the end that the promise should be sure to all the seed; not to the seed which is, from the Law only, the literal Jews, but also (which is now the salient point) to the seed which is from the faith of Abraham, the Gentiles. And thus, in God's plan, Abraham is held as father of us all, Gentiles as well as Jews.[35]

Henry W. Williams added,

> And thus, he maintains, the promise stands firm to all the spiritual seed of Abraham, — not only to those who share with him in the distinguishing rite of the ancient covenant, but to those who only tread in the steps of his faith. All true believers may look up to him as their father, and claim, in virtue of the promise made to him, a rich heritage of blessing.[36]

Romans 9:6

Romans 9-11 is the strongest sustained argument that covenant membership is not ethnic. Paul redefines Israel. The remnant consists of those Jews who put their faith in Jesus Christ. God's redemptive plan will not fail, but unbelieving Jews do not have covenant standing. The illustration of the olive tree teaches conditional, faith-based membership.

Binney explained, "Not all the natural descendants of

---

35 Williams, *Exposition*, 156.

36 Williams, *Exposition*, 114.

Israel are in spirit true Israelites."[37] Beet said that mass of Jews are outside the family of God, "So long as they continue in their present unbelief, they are outside the number of those for whom the promises were given."[38]

Wesley wrote, "The Jews imagined that the word of God must fail if all their nation were not saved. This St. Paul now refutes."[39] Clarke explained, "The Gentiles were included in the Abrahamic covenant as well as the Jews; and therefore the Jews have no exclusive right to the blessings of God's kingdom.[40] Benson noted that the Jews vehemently maintained that all who were born, and them only, were the people of God. But Paul here says the promises belong to "true spiritual Israelites," who have been born again by the supernatural power of God's Spirit and who by faith lay hold on the promise of salvation made in Christ — "these are they who are intended in the covenant with Abraham."[41]

Thomas Summers wrote,

> For not all who are lineally descended from Israel—the posterity of Jacob, the people called Israel—are "Israelites indeed," as there are those who say they are Jews—God's own people—and yet are not, but a synagogue of Satan. John 1:47; Rev. 2:9.[42]

---

[37]Binney, *The People's Commentary*, 416.

[38]Beet, *Romans*, 260.

[39]Wesley, *Notes*, 87.

[40]Clarke, *Commentary*, 6:110.

[41]Benson, *Notes*, 5:81-82.

[42]Summers, *Romans*, 148.

William Williams concluded that none of the explicit temporal blessings promised has ever been literally fulfilled. They were all conditional; and the conditions were never met by the unfaithful Jews.

> Clearly the covenant with the Jews was not "an everlasting covenant," unless in a figurative sense. It was often forsaken by the Jews, often repudiated by God, and finally abrogated. Clearly the land of Canaan was not "an everlasting possession." It never came into full possession of the Jews.[43]

Henry W. Williams wrote,

> Here the Apostle enters upon his great argument. Alluding to the fact that, under the constitution now brought in, the Jewish nation, as such, had ceased to be the visible Church of God, and that Church consisted only of those, whether Jews or Gentiles, who came to the Lord Jesus for gratuitous justification, and then openly confessed His Name, — he first affirms that this involved no failure of the Divine promise. And the position which he takes to prove it is, that the *mere* circumstance of natural descent from Israel had never been sufficient to constitute any man, in the highest sense, one of God's true Israel, — one of His covenant and accepted people.[44]

---

[43]William Williams, *Exposition*, 295.

[44]Williams, *Exposition*, 281.

Romans 10:12

Clarke wrote, "All are equally welcome to this salvation. Here the Jew has no exclusive privilege; and from this the Greek is not rejected. One simple way of being saved is proposed to all, [namely] faith in the Lord Jesus Christ."[45]

Here the apostle "reiterates the statement made in the third chapter of this Epistle . . . that there is no difference between the Jew and the Greek since all are placed under an economy of grace which offers to them, on the same simple condition of faith, the fullness of spiritual blessing.[46] "Whatever may have been the distinctions of the old election there is no difference or distinction here."[47]

Romans 11:26

The consensus of Methodist commentators is that there would be a future conversion of Israel. Wesley preached that the world would one day be "a Christian world," according to such passages as Romans 11:25-26.[48] He believed that a "grand Pentecost" will fully come.[49] Israel will be gathered into the Christian church, and universal holiness and happiness will be reestablished on earth. Wesley believed there will be a "vast harvest among the heathen." The resulting prosperity will provoke the Jews to jealousy. The Jewish people as a

---

[45]Clarke, *Commentary*, 6:122.

[46]Henry Williams, *Exposition*, 311-312.

[47]Burwash, *Romans*, 195.

[48]Wesley, "Scriptural Christianity," Sermon #4, 3.1-2.

[49]Wesley, "The General Spread of the Gospel," ¶ 20.

whole will be converted, "being convinced by the coming in of the gentiles. But there will be still a larger harvest among the Gentiles, when all Israel is come in."[50]

Benson said that although it has not yet happened, the conversion of the Jews appeared more probable than the conversion of the gentiles before they were converted.[51] If God can save a gentile, how much more can he save a Jew. Wesley wrote, "So many prophecies refer to this grand event, that it is surprising any Christian should doubt of it. And these are greatly confirmed by the wonderful preservation of the Jews, as a distinct people, to this day."

Wesley continued to say that this strong confirmation of biblical prophecy will convince many deists and nominal Christians. Their conversion will be the means of a swift propagation of the gospel among the Islamic and pagan world, "who would probably have received it long ago, had they conversed only with real Christians."[52] Binney wrote that "the general conversion of the Gentiles will not only precede, but largely contribute to bring about, the general conversion of the Jews."[53]

Sutcliffe wrote that Paul foresaw that the Jews would remain in unbelief, until Christian missionaries succeeded in largely converting the gentiles of every name and nation and

---

[50]Wesley, *Notes*, 395.

[51]Benson, *Notes*, 5:98.

[52]Wesley, *Notes*, 394. Benson included this entire paragraph [*Notes*, 5:95]. Coke made a very similar statement [*Commentary*, 6:122]. See also Outler in Wesley, *BE Works*, 1:90.

The equivalent to the eighteenth century deists would be the modernist or liberal who denies everything supernatural.

[53]Binney, *The People's Commentary*, 423.

in disseminating the holy Scriptures in every language. Then the veil would be taken away when providence illuminated prophecy. When this stumbling stone filled the whole earth, they would read their prophets with new eyes.[54]

Coke wrote that the future glory of the church, when the restoration of the Jews shall take place, will be like a resurrection from the dead (v 15). Therefore, we should pray for that great event — that the fullness of the gentiles may be brought in. So all Israel shall then be saved.[55] Coke also cited Romans 11:25 as plainly expressing the doctrine that there shall be such a happy period as the millennium.[56]

Nathaniel Burwash believed that vv 25-26 "express a firm faith in the salvation of the great majority of the race, *the fullness* of both Jew and gentile, and in the high perfection and spiritual power of the church, new "life from the dead," and in the glorious regeneration of humanity, "the riches of the world."[57]

Galatians 3:7

Wesley said that those who are partakers of Abraham's faith, "these, and these only, are the sons of Abraham."[58] "All who believe, as Abraham has believed, are made partakers of

---

[54]Sutcliffe, *Commentary*, 2:467.

[55]Coke, *Commentary*, 5:122, 127, 130.

[56]Coke, *Commentary*, 6:1004.

[57]Burwash, *Manual of Christian Theology on the Inductive Method*, 382-383.

[58]Wesley, *Notes*, 478.

Abraham's blessings."[59]

"Faith associates the believing gentile with all the family of the promised Seed, and makes him an heir of Abraham's covenant."[60] According to Whedon, Paul is saying, "Be well assured that faith makes you truer sons of Abraham than birth or circumcision."[61]

Galatians 3:28-29

Wesley said that there was no difference between Jew or Greek; "they are equally accepted through faith."[62] Under the gospel "all distinctions are done away . . . all are equally welcome to Christ, and all have an equal need of him."[63]

Benson wrote, "Under the gospel dispensation, God pays no regard to persons on account of their descent, their station, or their sex; but all who truly believe in Christ, have an equal right to the privileged of the gospel, are equally in favor with God, and are equal in respect and dignity."[64]

"All true believers show themselves to be the spiritual children of Abraham, and are blessed with him, their spiritual father."[65]

---

[59]Clarke, *Commentary*, 6:398.

[60]Sutcliffe, *Commentary*, 2:720.

[61]Whedon, *Commentary*, 4:225.

[62]Wesley, *Notes*, 480.

[63]Clarke, *Commentary*, 6:402.

[64]Benson, *Notes*, 5:283.

[65]Binney, *The People's Commentary*, 507.

Galatians 6:16

Clarke explained that true Christians are here called the Israel of God to distinguish them from Israel according to the flesh.[66]

The Israel of God is "the church of God; which consists of all those, and those only, of every nation and kindred, who walk by this rule."[67]

Amos Binney defined *the Israel of God* as being "True Christians, or Abraham's spiritual seed."[68]

Daniel Whedon explained,

> In this terse phrase Paul triumphantly embodies his great doctrine that the theocracy has left the old ritual and gone with the new Church of the Spirit.[69]

J. Agar Beet explained that *the Israel of God* either refers to the entire Church of God or the Jewish part of it. But Paul would not single out the Jews and raise them above their Gentile brethren when it has been his purpose in this whole letter to place them both on the same level.[70]

Ephesians 2:12-19

Benson said that Paul describes the conjunction of the

---

[66]Clarke, *Commentary*, 6:417.

[67]Wesley, *Notes*, 487. This is repeated by Benson, *Notes*, 5:297.

[68]Binney, *The People's Commentary*, 516.

[69]Whedon, *Commentary*, 4:249-250.

[70]Beet, *Galatians,* 177-178.

Gentiles with Israel in vv 14-15 and the conjunction of both with God in vv 16-18. The union of the Jews and the Gentiles, "so as to make them one people," was foretold by Jesus in John 10:16.[71] Jesus meant that the gentiles would be brought into one fold with the Jews. This is the teaching of Ephesians 2:14, that the wall between Jew and gentile has been broken down? Some dispensationalists would say that Jew and gentile share equally in salvation, but that this does not destroy the separate identities of Israel and the church. But what then is the creation of "one new man out of the two" (Eph 2:15), if the two retain their separate identities?

Clarke explained that the Church of God is compared to a city. "The Gentiles, having believed in Christ, are all incorporated with the believing Jews in this holy city."[72]

Philippians 3:3

In v 3, Paul defines the true Israel as those who worship by the Spirit of God, who glory in Christ alone, not trusting in themselves. They are the truly circumcised. Although the subject is implied in the Greek verb, here Paul adds the pronoun *hemeis* for emphasis. He also adds the article (*he*) which is not necessary. About the only way this can be conveyed in English is to write "we [alone] are the circumcised."

Thus, Wesley wrote, "Christians are the only true circumcision."[73] "We are the only people now in covenant with God,

---

[71]Benson, *Notes*, 5:310.

[72]Clarke, *Commentary*, 6:441.

[73]Wesley, *Notes*, 511.

who worship God in the Spirit."[74]

1 Peter 2:9

Peter described the church with four phrases. These titles come from Exodus 19 and Isaiah 43 where they were descriptions of Israel. Clarke wrote, "The titles formerly given to the whole Jewish Church, to all the Israelites without exception . . . are here given to Christians in general in the same way."[75] By applying them to the church, Peter is teaching that Gentiles now share in God's covenant with Israel. Whedon explained, "In a series of terms originally given to the literal Israel, and entirely applicable to the new and spiritual."[76] Binney wrote, "What God said of the literal Israel under the O. T. economy, holds good of the spiritual Israel under the New, embracing all of every nation who believe in Christ."[77] Wesley added, "In a higher sense than ever the Jews were."[78]

Revelation 3:9

The Jews were once God's chosen people, but they rejected their Messiah. For the second time Jesus called them the "synagogue of Satan" (2:9). Christians were locked out of the Jewish synagogue, but Christ said not to worry. Since he

---

[74]Benson, *Notes*, 5:351.

[75]Clarke, *Commentary*, 6:852.

[76]Whedon, *Commentary*, 5:202.

[77]Binney, *The People's Commentary*, 641.

[78]Wesley, *Notes*, 612,

holds the keys, they were only banned from the synagogue of Satan. He holds open the door of salvation and even the Jews will be drawn to Christ and will acknowledge that this little congregation is the true Israel of God and the inheritor of the promises to Abraham and Moses. Clarke wrote, "The love which was formerly fixed on the Jews is now removed, and transferred to the Gentiles."[79]

Whedon explained that these people were Jews "after the flesh; the which is now a nullity; but are not the spiritual Israel, which is now the only true Israel."[80]

---

[79]Clarke, *Commentary,* 6:984.

[80]Whedon, *Commentary,* 5:359.

Help from the Book of Hebrews

While dispensationalism tends to regard *replacement* as an inflammatory term, they bear the burden of proof to explain what is meant in the following passages:

- what is implied by *change* in 7:12?
- what does *nullify* mean in 7:18?
- what does 7:19 mean that a *better* hope has been introduced?
- what does 8:13 mean by saying that the old covenant is obsolete and will soon disappear?
- what does *set aside* connote in 10:9?

An inductive study of the Scripture reveals that there are eighteen descriptions of Israel given in the Old Testament which are transferred to the Christian church in the New Testament. There are also sixteen passages in the Old Testament referring to Israel which are quoted in the New Testament as referring to Christians. Both Old and New Testament saints make up the church, the bride of Christ, in Revelation 21:9-14. The New Jerusalem has twelve gates with the names of the twelve tribes of Israel. It has twelve foundations which contain the names of the twelve apostles. Therefore, the conditional privilege of old Israel has been transferred to the church. Jesus warned in the parable of the tenants that the vineyard would be taken away from those who neglected it and given to others (Luke 20:9-18). Yet Romans 11:26 foretells that they will be grafted back into the new covenant. But how could they be restored if they were never cut off?[81]

Three times in the book of Hebrews Jesus is identified as

---

[81]See Provan, *The Church is Israel Now.*

the mediator of the new covenant (Heb 8:6, 9:15, 12:24). While Hebrews 8 declares that the new covenant is *better*, there is still a continuity in God's covenants. They all contained law and grace. The difference between the old covenant, with its prescribed forms, and the new covenant, is a new life not a new prescription. Ezekiel 36:22-27 promised the enabling grace of the indwelling Spirit in order to keep the new covenant.

There are eight passages in Hebrews which must be processed in light of the controversy over "replacement theology":

- 1:1-2: the revelation of the Son is superior to the OT prophets, yet the writer relies heavily on OT passages to make that point.
- 3:7-4:13: Canaan or Palestine is not the final rest promised to God's people.
- the Aaronic priesthood has been set aside for the eternal priesthood of Christ.
- 8:5: the earthly sanctuary is merely a sketch and shadow of the heavenly sanctuary in which Jesus offered his perfect sacrifice.
- 8:8-13: the new covenant, as promised in Jeremiah 38:31-34, implies that the old one was somehow deficient.
- 10:4: states that the Old Testament sacrifices are inadequate.
- In chapter 11 the heroes of faith trusted in promises that were substantially unfulfilled under the old covenant. Faith under the former covenant is the same kind of faith that is required of believers under the new covenant — yet the object of New Testament faith is the atoning work of Jesus Christ.

- the warning passages, 2:1-4; 3:7-4:13; 6:4-8; 10:19-39; 12:14-29, which reference Israel's apostasy caution that for the Christian apostasy is even more serious.

A belief in progressive revelation or two covenants does not necessarily lead to dispensational theology. It was disingenuous for Walvoord to argue, "All theologians have some sort of a dispensational division if no more than to divide the Old and New Testament." Walvoord then quoted Chafer who said, "Anyone is a dispensationalist who no longer offers lambs on brazen altars or who does not observe Saturday as the day of rest."[82]

Richard S. Taylor wrote that dispensationalists see numerous covenants, but the New Testament recognizes only two: the one before Christ and the one since Christ.[83] In fact, there is both continuity and discontinuity. However, the new covenant is *better*. It encapsulates key promises in earlier covenants but transcends them through the enabling of the Holy Spirit. The new covenant also incorporates Gentiles into the church, making them the joint-heirs of Old Testament promises. It is dispensationalism which insists Israel and the church must be kept separate.

> The author writes of Christianity as the final religion, not because he regards the faith of the OT as mistaken, but because he sees it as God's way of pointing men to Jesus. Judaism is not so much abrogated by Christianity as brought to its climax. The fuller meaning of the OT is to be seen in the person

---

[82]Walvoord, "Dispensational Premillennialism," 11-13.

[83]Taylor, *BBC*, 10:93.

and work of Jesus.[84]

Since the old covenant is null and void, the ethnic Jew is no better nor any worse than the rest of the human race. He will be saved by grace through faith in Jesus Christ, just like every other sinner. And the good news is that all Israel will be saved (Rom 11:26).

---

[84]Morris, "Hebrews," 7.

Covenant Theology

In his *Dictionary*, Richard Watson wrote that there are really only two covenants: the covenant of works and the covenant of grace. Watson taught that after Adam broke the covenant of works, God gave Abraham a covenant of grace. While the Mosaic dispensation was also a covenant of works, it was given to demonstrate man's sinfulness and was a foreshadowing of something better. Like the covenant with Adam, the covenant with Moses was broken by Israel and ended by God. The new covenant, argued Watson, was really the substance of the Abrahamic covenant.[85]

God made a covenant with Abraham, which was expanded under Moses, and again under David. The blessing of the covenant was that all the world would receive a Savior through the Jews. The Jews, however, misunderstood that they were God's unconditional elect — regardless of whether or not they kept the terms of the covenant.

When the Jews rejected Jesus the Messiah, this covenant was broken. We are now under a new covenant which includes all who trust in Jesus as Savior — regardless of whether they are Jew or Gentile.

Theologically, one of the most basic concept is that covenants contain conditions. Wesley explained that the covenant made with Abraham was everlasting, but it was also conditional.[86] The terms are everlasting, but there are stipulations. There are blessings for those who keep the covenant and punishment for those who break it. However, John MacArthur insisted that God's covenant with Abraham was unilateral,

---

[85]Watson, *Biblical and Theological Dictionary*, 273-274.

[86]Wesley, *BE Works*, 13:297-298.

unconditional, sovereign, and irrevocable.[87]

According to Hebrews 8:9 the Israelites broke the covenant, and so God annulled or disregarded it (*ameleo*). The abrogation and replacement of the old covenant with something better in v 10 certainly supports the concept of replacement.

The Hebrews writer urges his readers to go outside the camp (13:13) — to distinguish themselves from those who still live by the provisions of the old order. "This is a summons to break with Judaism and to serve Christ."[88] According to Wesley we are exhorted to go forth "out of the Jewish dispensation."[89] Christ abolished the old order (7:18). Christianity has superceded Judaism. The church has superceded Israel. Dods wrote that the aim of the writer is to prove that the old covenant is superceded by the new.[90]

This conclusion, however, is rejected by dispensationalism as "replacement theology." The more academic term is *supersessionism*. Dispensationalists claim that God's covenant with Israel is unconditional and therefore he cannot break his word. However, to impose this theological debate on the text of Hebrews is wrong. Hebrews, with its interpretation of God's covenantal dealings with Israel, refutes a dispensational reading. While God will not break his Word, if we break covenant with God the covenant is null and void.

We must recognize both a continuity and discontinuity. The butterfly does not exactly replace the caterpillar. It is a new phase of existence which actually surpasses the caterpil-

---

[87]Waldron, *MacArthur's Millennial Manifesto*, 152-164.

[88]Rushdoony, *Hebrews, James, and Jude*, 1.

[89]Wesley, *Notes*, 594.

[90]Dods, "Hebrews," 247.

lar. The church is a continuation and expansion of Israel, not necessarily a replacement. Oden explained, "The new Israel does not destroy but fulfills the promise of the old."[91]

John MacArthur, however, claimed that if the church replaced Israel, that would presuppose an Arminian view of election. He declared, "If you get Israel right you will get eschatology right. If you don't get Israel right, you will never get eschatology right." Thus, he argued for premillennialism.[92] He should have specified *dispensational* premillennialism. However, the "error" he wants to avoid is preferable to the error he creates.

Israel is depicted as the flock of God in Psalm 78:52-55, 80:1-3, Isaiah 40:9-11, Jeremiah 23:1-3, 31:10-12, Ezekiel 34:12-16, Micah 5:1-4, Zechariah 10:3-5. According to Hebrews 13:20-21 Jesus Christ is the great Shepherd of the sheep. Do the Father and the Son have two different flocks?

According to Numbers 12:1-9, Israel is the house of God. But Hebrews 3:1-6, 10:21-22 says Christians are the house of God. Do the Father and the Son have two different houses?

Jerusalem is the city and mother of Israel in Psalm 149:2, Isaiah 12:6, 49:18-22, 51:18, Lamentations 4:2. In Hebrews 12:22 Jerusalem is the city and mother of Christians.

According to Jeremiah 31:31-33 the new covenant is with Israel. According to Hebrews 8:8-12 it is with Christians. In order to salvage their dispensational assumptions, both Walvoord and Ryrie teach two new covenants.[93]

In Deuteronomy 31:6 Moses told Israel, "He will never

---

[91]Oden, *Life in the Spirit*, 269.

[92]Waldron, *MacArthur's Millennial Manifesto*, 145-146.

[93]Walvoord, *The Millennial Kingdom*, 209-214; Ryrie, *Basis of the Premillennial Faith*, 107.

leave you nor forsake you." Hebrews 13:5 makes the same promise to Christians.

Deuteronomy 32:36 and Psalm 135:14 promise that the Lord will judge his people. The same statement is made in Hebrews 10:30. Thus, Christians are now his people.

In Psalm 22:22 Christ is prophesied to declare God's name to his brothers who are Jewish. But in Hebrews 2:12 Christ's brothers are Christians.

Psalm 95:7-11 warns that Israel will never enter into God's rest. Hebrews 3:7-11 warns that Christians who go back will never enter into God's rest.

The author of Hebrews quotes a passage in Isaiah 35:3 that is referring to Jews on their way to Zion and in 12:12 applies it to Christians.

False Conclusions Based on False Interpretations

Because we have not worked through these issues in a consistent and systematic method, the Jews are blamed for everything wrong in the world by some conspiracy theorists, while dispensationalists regard God's plan for Israel as a distinct tract from his plan for the church. Ultra-conservative "right wing" politics hates Israel as the one-world government conspiracy. Ultra-liberal "left wing" politics hate Israel primarily over their human rights violations.

At this point we must define *liberal* and *conservative.* They are both neutral terms used relative to the subject. The word *liberal* defines one who loves liberty. However, when the French Revolution rebelled against God, *liberals* became those who rejected God and his law and replaced God with human reason.

On the other hand a *conservative* defines one who wants to preserve traditional social, cultural, and political institutions. If those traditions are based on a Judeo-Christian ethic, then I am a conservative. If I lived under Soviet communism I would be a liberal. And every conservative pastor still appreciates a liberal offering! My point is not to be evasive. However, liberal sinners and conservative sinners are both wrong.[94] The biblical answer is *radical.* This is another loaded term. *Radical* actually means something that goes to the root, origin, or core of a subject. In this case our starting point, our root or origin or core, is Scripture. This is what the Protestants mean by the Latin term *sola Scriptura.*

What follows are both liberal and conservative distor-

[94]I am not implying that everyone I disagree with in this section is not a Christian. I am stating categorically, however, that everyone who teaches racial hatred is *not* a Christian.

tions of what Scripture teaches;

- British Israelism (also called Anglo-Israelism) is a belief that the people of Great Britain are genetically, racially, and linguistically the direct descendants of the Ten Lost Tribes of ancient Israel. British Israelism was inspired by several 19th-century English writings such as John Wilson's 1840 *Lectures On Our Israelitish Origin*. From the 1870s onward, numerous independent British Israelite organizations were set up throughout the British Empire as well as in the United States; as of the early 21st century, a number of these organizations are still active. In the United States, the idea gave rise to the Christian Identity movement which is antisemitic and white supremacist.[95]

- Zionism is the movement for the return of the Jewish people to their ancient homeland. This idea was first articulated by Theodor Herzl in 1896. It was advanced through the Balfour Declaration in 1917 and implemented in 1948 when the state of Israel was founded.

Therefore, dispensationalism insists that the United States must unconditionally support the political state of Israel.[96] According to dispensationalism there will even be a

---

[95]"Christian Identity," *Watchman Fellowship Profile*, 1999. Roberts, "Race Over Grace," 11-14. I heard Gene Scott teach this over the radio when I lived in Los Angeles.

[96]Timothy P. Weber, "How Evangelicals Became Israel's Best Friend," Christianity Today, 5 Oct, 1998, p. 41. See also Weber, "Dispensationalists Organize to Support Israel," chapter 8 of *On*

separate judgment dealing with how the nations treated Israel.[97] However, I do not unconditionally support anything or anyone except Jesus Christ and the teachings of Scripture.

However, the promises of land to Israel were conditional, according to Leviticus 18:24-30. Dispensationalism has embraced a Zionism which declares that God has forever given Palestine to the political nation of Israel. While land was promised in Genesis 12:1, that promise was conditional, and the promise was fulfilled in Joshua 21:43-45. Thus, the promise is not eternal.[98]

Land was never the focus, however. Spiritual rest from the wanderings of sin is the promise. Eternal rest is promised to those who keep covenant. Palestine is not "the holy land." God has promised that the meek will inherit the whole earth, not just the mid-East. Stephen Sizer concluded,

> Christian Zionists appear to read the Old Testament in the same way that the first disciples did before Pentecost, believing the coming of the kingdom of Jesus meant a postponement of Jewish hopes for restoration rather than the fulfilment of those hopes in the Messiah and his new and inclusive Messianic community.[99]

Nothing in the New Testament says anything about a rebuilt temple. There is no need for one because the temple

---

the Road to Armageddon.

[97] *New Scofield Reference Bible,* 859.

[98] Sizer, *Christian Zionism*, 155; Gentry, *He Shall Have Dominion*, 190-192.

[99] Sizer, *Christian Zionism*, 259.

was always planned for obsolescence. Jesus was the temple (John 2:13-22). He was "the door" (10:7, 9) and the "chief cornerstone" (Matt. 21:42; Acts 4:11; Eph. 2:20; 1 Pet 2:6). Jesus serves as the High Priest and Mediator between God and humanity.

- "Replacement theology"

Dispensationalists claim that God's covenant with Israel is unconditional, and therefore he cannot break his word. Thus, Palestine is unconditionally promised to the Jews forever. They reject covenant theology as "replacement" theology. This pejorative label is discussed throughout this book.

- The Hebrew Roots Movement is a Christian-based, Torah-observant movement that advocates for adhering to the Mosaic Law while recognizing Jesus (often called Yeshua) as the Messiah. Followers believe that the Law of Moses was not abolished and that Christians should observe the seventh-day Sabbath, biblical feasts, and dietary laws. They need to realize that Jesus has ended the old Jewish economy.

Furthermore, I am not interested in debating with Nehemia Gordon the proper Hebrew pronunciation of the name *God* or *Jesus.* Jews use the word *abba* and gentiles use the word *pater*, but if they have faith in Jesus they are praying to the same God (Rom 8:15). And he hears them in every language.

- Jewish conspiracy theories

The Protocols of the Elders of Zion taught an international Jewish conspiracy. It was first published in 1903. It claims Jews manipulate global financial systems, control the press, and infiltrate governments. This will result in Armageddon, which is misinterpreted as a race war. There is a heavy emphasis on how to survive. False doctrine based on the book of Genesis leads to a false eschatology when these errors are applied to the book of Revelation.

While pastoring in western Kansas in the late 1970s-early 1980s, I came in contact with paramilitary organizations who had radio programs on KTTL in Dodge City.[100] As a pastor, I spoke out about what was being taught. I have no idea what was the scope of this movement.[101] However, the station was playing tapes supplied by James Wickstrom and Rev. William Potter Gale, the founder of the California-based Ministry of Christ Church and the virtual leader of what is known as the Identity movement. I heard them teach that Jews were only 5/8 human. This odd fraction stems from calculations combining two core tenets of the movement: Pre-Adamite Theology and the Two-Seedline Doctrine. Without delving deeply into this folk theology, it has been taught that all non-whites descended from a preAdam race. This notion is coupled with the gap theory of Genesis 1:1-2, also called the ruin-redemption theory.[102] The notion of preadamic mankind is actually a

---

[100]See O'Shaughnessy, "'Patriots' ready for final fight;" Verdon, "Couple take heat for radio broadcasts;" "Radio station plans to continue airing tapes."

[101]See Abanes, *America's Militias* for the broader picture.

[102]*Dake Annotated Reference Bible*, 54. See also, Dake, *Another Time, Another Place* (1977). This teaching was also promoted by Larkin [*Dispensational Truth*, 7; 111], as well as the Scofield Reference Bible. To be clear not everyone who accepts the "gap

contradiction, since *adam* is a generic term for original humanity. According to Acts 17:26 every ethnicity stems from one common man — Adam. However, if people believe that there was a creation prior to Adam this truth can be distorted.

In 1878 Alexander Winchell wrote *Adamites and Pre-Adamites: A Popular Discussion Concerning the Remote Representations of the Human Species and their Relation to the Biblical Adam*. He argued that preadamites were intellectually and culturally inferior to Adamites. He claimed that people of color would never reach the intellectual capacity of white populations.[103]

As recently as 1947 Theodore G. Bilbo devoted an entire chapter in his book, *Take Your Choice: Separation or Mongrelization*, devoted an entire chapter, chapter 8, of his 330 page book to refute Acts 17:26.[104]

The two-seedline doctrine is also called the serpent's seed doctrine. It holds that Eve had sexual relations with the

---

theory" also affirms the teaching of a preAdamic race. However, Scofield, Larkin, and Dake affirmed both. Incredibly, Gleason Archer also accepted both [*Survey of Old Testament Introduction*, 198-199].

[103]Apparently, Whedon entertained the notion of a preadamic and prehistoric creation, but ultimately rejected the theory [Miley, *Systematic Theology*, 1:391-392]. Whedon reviewed *Adamites and Pre-Adamites* by Alexander Winchell in the July 1878 issue of the *Methodist Quarterly Review*. Winchell was dismissed from the faculty of Vanderbilt University as a result of this book.

[104]Bilbo served two-terms as the Democrat governor of Mississippi and later was elected to the U. S. Senate. His argument was that the brotherhood of mankind is to be understood spiritually, not physically. This is "proven" by nature and history. It is also a poor hermeneutic.

serpent, or Satan. Cain the result. Cain and his offspring intermarried with the preAdamites resulting in a "mongrel" race now known as the Jews. Pentecostal evangelist William Branham taught that Eve had sex with Satan and this was the original sin. This illicit sex was the forbidden fruit and the result was Cain.[105] However, white supremacists claim that Cain was cursed and that curse was marked by his black skin. But Genesis 4:15 does not teach this racism.

Another variation, building on British-Israelism, is that Cain was the father of the Jews.[106] The Christian Identity Movement also believes that other races descended from human beings created before Adam. Thus, only Whites are the true Israel and the true descendants of Adam. This provides a pseudo-biblical basis for racism. In many ways it is the polar opposite of the Zionist movement.

This nonsense is protected free speech since it incorporates the Bible, is thus "religious," and is preached by such "Reverends" as Gale. However, it seldom makes it on the radar of more academic theologians who are more geared to reading books. Yet at a grass-roots level, on the other side of the tracks, it has been taught for a hundred years or more.

Charles Parham, the "projector" of the Pentecostal movement which began in 1901, accepted the British Israel

---

[105]Branham, "The Original Sin." See also Liardon, *God's Generals*, 339-340. Branham was illiterate and therefore wrote no books. He died in 1965 but has more theological influence today than then. He influenced prominent figures, including Paul Cain, who later brought this prophetic focus to John Wimber and the Vineyard Movement and the birth of the New Apostolic Reformation.

[106]Abanes, *American Militias*, 162.

theory.[107] He became involved in support of the Ku Klux Klan.[108] Throughout Parham's life he advocated white supremacy based on his theology of Anglo-Saxon superiority as the ten lost tribes of Israel (also called British Israelism). He supported racial segregation on the basis of two creations: those created on the sixth day were created in God's image; the Adamic race was formed on the eighth day. The punishment of the Noahic flood was because the sixth day creation had intermarried with the eighth day creation.[109]

Tragically, some unemployed young men are told by influencers such as Nick Fuentes that the reason they cannot find a decent job is because of this Jewish conspiracy. Charlie Kirk, in particular, met this scapegoating head on.

- Dual-covenant theology

John Hagee holds that Jewish people do not need to be saved since they are under a different covenant.[110] While Hagee told the Jerusalem Post and Baptist Press that he does not believe in or teach dual-covenant theology Hagee teaches

---

[107]Parham, *Sermons: Voice Crying in the Wilderness*, 20; 105-108; *Everlasting Gospel*, 92-95; 111-117. See also Hollenweger, *Pentecostals*, 22; Cargill, *How God Communicates with Man*, 38.

[108]Parham, *Sermons: Everlasting Gospel*, 91-110; 115-118.See also Synan, *Holiness-Pentecostal Tradition*, 182; Goff, *Fields White Unto Harvest*, 128-132; Grady, "Pentecostals Renounce Racism," 58.

[109]Callahan, "Fleshly Manifestations," chapter 3, "Azusa's Shame: Racial Boundaries and Apostolic Faith," 101-140.

[110]House, "Summary Critique,"50-52. Hummel, *The Rise and Fall of Dispensationalism*, 295-296.

that the covenant God made with Abraham is everlasting and not superseded by Christianity. Hagee's organization, Christians United for Israel (CUFI), focuses on political support for Israel rather than converting Jewish people, suggesting that the Jewish relationship with God is unique. He makes it a practice not to target Jews for conversion at his "Night to Honor Israel" events.

In Defense of Israel, Hagee teaches that God's covenant with the Jewish people is eternal, unconditional, and never replaced by the Christian church.[111]

This two-covenant theology holds that Gentiles are saved by faith in Christ while Jews are saved by keeping the law. However, Paul prayed for Israel "that they may be saved" (Rom 10:1-2), instead of insisting that they already were. Salvation has always been by grace through faith.

- The curse on the Jews

Matt 27:25 Regarding "his blood be upon us and upon our children," Wesley said, "This imprecation was dreadfully answered in the ruin so quickly brought on the Jewish nation, and in the calamities which have ever since pursued that wretched people."[112]

Someday that curse will turn to blessing as all Israel is saved (Rom 11:26). In the meantime we have no command to enforce judgment. According to Deuteronomy 24:16 and Ezekiel 18:20 we should not punish people for the sins of their ancestors.

---

[111]Hagee, *In Defense of Israel* (2007). See Gentry, "In Defense of Zionism: Hagee's Mandate for Supporting Israel," 48-49,

[112]Wesley, *Notes*, 92.

During the Middle Ages the church tended to treat Jews with "hatred and disdain."[113] Towards the end of his life, Martin Luther made inflammatory statements in his book *On the Jews and Their Lies* (1543). The Nazis reprinted these statements in 1938 as justification for their brutal agenda. Instead of punishing them we should preach the gospel to them, but it does more harm than good to do both!

- Rapture theories

Charles Ryrie insisted that it is mandatory for dispensationalists to separate Israel and the church. He said this distinction between Israel and the church is probably the most basic theological test of whether or not a person is dispensational.[114] This insistence on discontinuity has led dispensationalism to interject a secret rapture of the church into God's plan, so that God could revert back to Israel. Walvood explained, "It is therefore not too much to say that the rapture question is determined more by ecclesiology than eschatology."[115] Thus, the rapture is only for the church and the millennium only for Israel.

Three Greek words, *parousia*, *apokalupsis*, and *epiphaneia* are all utilized to describe one great future event. Those who make a distinction between the *rapture* and the *revelation* or *return* of Jesus Christ also base their teaching on the use of three Greek words. *Parousia* is said to refer to the

---

[113]Schaff, *History of the Christian Church*, 5:443.

[114]Ryrie, *Dispensationalism Today*, 44-45; see also 47, 96, 159.

[115]Walvoord, *The Rapture Question*, 15-16. This concession is found in the 1957 original edition, but was expunged from subsequent editions from 1970-1979.

rapture and *apokalupsis* and *ephiphaneia* are said to refer to the revelation. However, in 2 Thessalonians 2:8 both *parousia* and *ephiphaneia* are used in the same verse to describe the same event. If this artificial distinction is followed, the *blessed hope* promised in Titus 2:13-14 would not be the rapture since the word *ephiphaneia* is used. This is also true of 2 Timothy 4:8.

Some also say Christ must first come *for* his saints in the rapture and then after a disputed length of time come *with* his saints in revelation. They use 1 Thessalonians 3:13 as a proof text since it uses the word *with*. However, the Greek word used is *parousia*, and by their definition this word refers to the rapture. John Walvoord conceded this point. Most dispensationalists changed their presentation, but not their conclusions, in the 1940s.[116]

First Thessalonians 4:15-17 is the most commonly used passage to support the idea of a secret rapture. I affirm what it teaches, but I deny that it teaches a secret return of Christ for his church which may be as long as seven years before his second advent. The text does compare his coming to a thief who comes unexpectedly, but nothing about this coming is secret. On the contrary, it will be loud enough to raise the dead! Proof-texts for the rapture are usually describing the general resurrection, not a secret rapture. The blessed hope, described in Titus 2:13, is not a secret rapture, but the visible appearing of Jesus Christ at the end of time. When he returns no one will be left behind.[117]

Not only do premillennialists disagree as to whether this rapture is to be pre-trib, mid-trib, post-trib, or pre-wrath, but

---

[116]Walvoord, "New Testament Words for the Lord's Coming," 284-289; Reiter, "Development of the Rapture Positions," 30.

[117]Reasoner, "What 'Left Behind' Left Out," 9-11.

some teach a partial rapture in which only those members of their select group will miss the tribulation period. After surveying the major passages used to prove two phases to Christ's return, George Eldon Ladd summarized his findings:

> The vocabulary used of our Lord's return lends no support for the idea of two comings of Christ or of two aspects of his coming. On the contrary it substantiates the view that the return of Christ will be a single, indivisible, glorious event.[118]

Christ declared that "the wheat and the tares are to remain together in the field until the harvest" or end of the age. The secret rapture theory, however, teaches that all the wheat is removed and the tares left standing before the end. We are assured that Christ will come "the second time without sin unto salvation" (Heb 9:28), but there is no clear teaching scripturally that he will come a third or fourth time. In contrast to premilennial speculation, W. B. Pope declared, "There is but one visible appearance of Christ set before the expectation of His people."[119]

Thus, one error necessitates another error. A misunderstanding about God's plan for Israel has created a whole rapture theology that is not taught in Scripture but is a logical necessity if you accept the dispensation premise.

---

[118]Ladd, *The Last Things*, 57; *The Blessed Hope*, 70. See also Wiley, *Christian Theology*, 3:250.

[119]Pope, *Compendium*, 3:399.

Conclusion

Unless we can sort out Israel's identity biblically we can end up with a secular Israel who rejects the Messiah but is treated as privileged according to God's old covenant with Israel. Conversely, an Arab Christian who has the faith of Abraham is discriminated against. A Messianic Jew who has embraced Abraham's faith is viewed with suspicion by secular Jews. And a Gentile convert to Judaism with no Jewish DNA is treated as a recipient of old covenant blessing. And a bloodline Jew who believes in Christ does not get a bonus. He shares the same blessing as the Gentile who believes in Christ.

I have tried to fellowship with true believers, whatever their denomination. I have received pushback, however, by asking whether those who hold classic Methodist doctrine are welcome in new Methodist organizations. Although I have been disenfranchised, I gather that they were more interested in Karl Barth than in John Wesley.

At this point I must ask the same question of those who are in more conservative holiness denominations. They have extended the cold shoulder of no fellowship to those who reject their fear mongering. They have embraced an alien dispensational theology and believe that they have "improved" on the theology of John Wesley. They reprinted all the writings of Daniel Steele, but followed the doctrine of John Darby.

BIBLIOGRAPHY

Abanes, William J. *America's Militias*. Downers Grove, IL: InterVarsity, 1996

Ardnt, William F. and F. Wilbur Gingrich. *A Greek-English Lexicon of the New Testament*. 2nd ed. Chicago: University of Chicago Press, 1979.

Allis, Oswald T. *Prophecy and the Church*. Philadelphia: Presbyterian & Reformed, 1945.

Archer, Gleason L. Jr. *A Survey of Old Testament Introduction*. Moody, 1974.

Arminius, James. *The Works of James Arminius*. 3 vols. The London Edition. 1825-1875. Reprint, Grand Rapids: Baker, 1996.

Barclay, William. *The Daily Study Bible Series: The Letter to the Romans*. Revised ed. Philadelphia: Westminster, 1975.

Bass, Clarence B. *Backgrounds to Dispensationalism: Its Historical Genesis and Ecclesiastical Implications*. 1960. Reprint, Grand Rapids: Baker, 1977.

Beet, Joseph Agar. *A Commentary on St. Paul's Epistle to the Romans*. 10th ed. 1902. Reprint, Salem, OH: Allegheny, 1982.

__________. *Commentary on St. Paul's Epistle to the Galatians*. 7th ed. 1897. Reprint, Salem, OH: Schmul, 1981.

Benson, Joseph. *The Holy Bible, with Notes, All the Marginal Readings, Summaries, and the Date of Every Transaction*. 2nd ed. 5 vols. 1811-1815. Reprint, New York: Carlton & Phillips, 1856.

Bilbo, Theodore G. *Take Your Choice: Separation or Mongrelization*. Popularville, MS: Dream House, 1957.

Binney, Amos and Daniel Steele. *The People's Commentary*. New York: Eaton & Mains, 1878.

Boyd, Alan Patrick. "A Dispensational Premillennial Analysis of the Eschatology of the Post-Apostolic Fathers (Until the Death of Justin Martyr)," Unpublished master's thesis, Dallas Theological Seminary, 1977.

Branham, William. "The Original Sin." http://www.williambranham.com/the-original-sin

Bray, Gerald, ed. *Ancient Christian Commentary on Scripture: Romans.* Downers Grove, IL: InterVarsity, 1998.

Burwash, Nathaniel. *A Handbook of the Epistle of St. Paul to the Romans.* 2nd ed. Toronto: William Briggs, 1900.

Callahan, Leslie Dawn. "Fleshly Manifestations: Charles Fox Parham's Quest for the Sanctified Body." PhD diss: Princeton University, 2002.

Cargill, A. L. *How God Communicates with Man or the Tongues Error.* Florence, CO: Wells of Baca, 1975.

"Christian Identity," *Watchman Fellowship Profile*, 1999.

Clarke, Adam. *The Holy Bible, Containing the Old and New Testaments: The Text Carefully Printed from the Most Correct Copies of the Present Authorized Translations, Including the Marginal reading and Parallel Tests; with a Commentary and Critical Notes, Designed as a help to a Better Understanding of the Sacred Writings.* 6 vols. 1811-1825. Reprint, Nashville: Abingdon, 1950.

Coke, Thomas. *A Commentary on the Holy Bible.* 6 vols. London: G. Whitfield, 1801-1803.

Dake, Finis J. *Dake Annotated Study Bible.* Lawrenceville, GA: Dake Bible Sales, 1963.

__________. *Another Time, Another Place.* Mark Allison and David Patton, eds. Lawrenceville, GA: Dake Publishing, 1997.

"Daniel Told Us! Adam Clarke Showed Us," *Faith in the Future* 23:4 (April, 1995).

Dods, Marcus. "Hebrews." *The Expositor's Greek Testament.* Vol 4. W. Robertson Nicoll, ed. 1897. Reprint, Eerdmans,

1983.
Dunning, H. Ray. *Grace, Faith, and Holiness.* Kansas City: Beacon Hill, 1988.
Earle, Ralph. *What the Bible Says About the Second Coming.* 1970. Reprinted, Grand Rapids: Baker, 1973.
Falwell, Jerry with Ed Dobson and Ed Hindson. *The Fundamentalist Phenomenon.* Garden City, NY: Doubleday, 1981.
Gentry, Kenneth L. Jr. *He Shall Have Dominion.* Tyler, TX: Institute for Christian Economics, 1992.
_________. "In Defense of Zionism: Hagee's Mandate for Supporting Israel." *Christian Research Journal* 31:4 (2008) 48-49.
Goff, James M, Jr. *Fields White Unto Harvest: Charles F. Parham and the Missionary Origins of Pentecostalism.* Fayetteville, AR: University of Arkansas, 1988.
Godet, Frederick. *Commentary on the Epistle to the Romans.* 1883. Reprint, Grand Rapids: Zondervan, 1956.
Grady, J. Lee. "Pentecostals Renounce Racism." *Christianity Today* 38:14 (12 Dec 1994) 58.
Gregg, Steve. *There Is Another King.* Book One of *Empire of the Risen Son.* Maitland, FL: Xulon, 2020.
Hanna, Mark M. "Israel Today: What Place in Prophecy?" *Christianity Today* 26:2 (22 January 1982) 14-17.
Hagee, John. *In Defense of Israel: The Bible's Mandate for Supporting the Jewish State.* Lake Mary, FL: Frontline, 2007.
Hollenweger, Walter J. *The Pentecostals.* Minneapolis: Augsburg, 1972.
House, H. Wayne. "A Summary Critique: Beginning of the End." *Christian Research Journal* 19:3 (Winter 1997) 50-52.
Hummel, Daniel G. *The Rise and Fall of Dispensationalism.* Grand Rapids: Eerdmans, 2023.
Justin Martyr. "Dialogue with Trypho, a Jew." *The Apostolic*

Fathers with Justin Martyr and Irenaeus. A Cleveland Coxe, ed. 1885. Reprint, Grand Rapids: Eerdmans, 1979.

Ladd, George Eldon. "Historic Premillennialism." *The Meaning of the Millennium: Four Views.* Robert G. Clouse, ed. Downers Grove, IL: InterVarsity, 1977.

_________. *The Blessed Hope.* Grand Rapids: Eerdmans, 1956.

_________. *The Last Things.* Grand Rapids: Eerdmans, 1978.

Larkin, Clarence. *Dispensational Truth.* Philadelphia: Clarence Larkin Estate, 1918.

Liardon, Roberts. *God's Generals.* Tulsa: Albury, 1996.

McClintock, John and James Strong. *Cyclopedia of Biblical, Theological, and Ecclesiastical Literature.* 12 vols. 1867-1887. Reprint, Grand Rapids: Baker, 1981.

Miley, John. *Systematic Theology.* 2 vols. 1893. Reprint, Peabody, MA: Hendrickson, 1989.

Morris, Leon. "Hebrews." *The Expositor's Bible Commentary.* Vol 12. Frank E. Gaebelein, ed. Zondervan, 1981.

Oden, Thomas C. *Life in the Spirit: Systematic Theology: Volume Three.* San Francisco: HarperCollins, 1992.

O'Shaughnessy, Lynn. "'Patriots' ready for final fight." *The Kansas City Times* (21 Nov 1981) A-1, A-9.

Parham, Charles F. *The Sermons of Charles F. Parham: A Voice Crying in the Wilderness.* 1911. Reprint, New York: Garland, 1985.

Pope, William Burt. *A Compendium of Christian Theology.* 3 vols. London: Wesleyan Conference Office, 1880.

Provan, Charles D. *The Church is Israel Now.* Vallecito, CA: Ross House, 1987.

"Radio station plans to continue airing tapes," *Dodge City Daily Globe* (5 Oct 1983).

Reasoner, Vic. "What 'Left Behind' Left Out," *The Arminian Magazine* 19:1 (Spring 2001) 9-11.

Reiter, Richard R. "A History of the Development of the Rapture Positions." *The Rapture: Pre-, Mid-, or Post-Tribulational?* Grand Rapids: Zondervan, 1984.

Roberts, Charles H. "Race Over Grace: Why Christian Identity Has It Wrong." *Biblical Worldview* (April 2005) 11-14.

Rushdoony, Rousas John. *Hebrews, James, and Jude*. Ross House, 2001.

Ryrie, Charles C. *The Basis of the Premillennial Faith*. Neptune, NJ: Loizeaux Brothers, 1953.

__________. *Dispensationalism Today*. Chicago: Moody, 1965.

Schaff, Philip. *History of the Christian Church*. 8 vols. 5th ed. 1889. Reprint, Grand Rapids: Eerdmans, 1980.

Scofield, C. I., ed. *New Scofield Reference Bible*. New York: Oxford, 1967.

Simon, Merrill. *Jerry Falwell and the Jews*. Middle Village, NY: Jonathan David Publishers, 1984.

Sizer, Stephen. *Christian Zionism*. Downers Grove, IL: InterVarsity, 2004.

Snodgrass, Klyne. *Ephesians: The NIV Application Commentary*. Grand Rapids: Zondervan, 1996.

Steele, Daniel. *A Substitute for Holiness; or Antinomianism Revived*. 3rd ed. 1899. [1st edition 1887] Reprint, Salem, OH: Schmul 1980. This was first reprinted under the title *Steele's Answers*.

Summers, Thomas O. *The Epistle of Paul, the Apostle, to the Romans, in the Authorized Version; with a New Translation and Commentary.* Nashville: Southern Methodist Publishing House, 1881.

Sutcliffe, Joseph. *A Commentary on the Old and New Testament*. 2 vols. London: Holdsworth and Ball, 1834.

Synan, Vinson. *The Holiness-Pentecostal Tradition: Charismatic Movements in the Twentieth Century*. Grand Rapids: Eerdmans, 1997.

Taylor, Richard S. "Hebrews." *Beacon Bible Commentary*. Vol

10. Beacon Hill, 1967.
Verdon, Roger. "Couple take heat for radio broadcasts," *The Hutchinson News* (23 June 1985).
Waldron, Samuel E. *MacArthur's Millennial Manifesto.* Owensboro, KY: RBAP, 2008.
Walvoord, John F. "Dispensational Premillennialism." *Christianity Today* 2:24 (15 September 1958) 11-13.
_________. *The Millennial Kingdom.* 1959. Reprint, Grand Rapids: Zondervan, 1994.
_________. *The Rapture Question.* Findlay, OH: Dunham, 1957.
_________. "New Testament Words for the Lord's Coming." *Bibliotheca Sacra* 101 (July-September 1944) 283-289.
Watson, Richard. *A Biblical and Theological Dictionary.* New York: Carlton & Porter, 1832.
_________. *An Exposition of the Gospels of St. Matthew and St. Mark.* London: Wesleyan Conference Office, 1833.
_________. *Sermons and Sketches of Sermons.* 2 vols. New York: Carlton & Porter, 1851.
Weber, Timothy P. "How Evangelicals Became Israel's Best Friend." *Christianity Today* 42:11 (5 Oct 1998) 38-49.
_________. "Dispensationalists Organize to Support Israel," chapter 8 of *On the Road to Armageddon.* Grand Rapids: Baker, 2004.
Wesley, John. *The Bicentennial Edition of the Works of John Wesley.* Randy Maddox, 35 volumes when complete. Nashville: Abingdon, 1976-.
_________. *Explanatory Notes Upon the New Testament.* 1754. Reprint, Salem, OH: Schmul, 1976.
Whedon, Daniel D. *Commentary on the New Testament.* 5 vols. 1860-1880. Reprint, Salem, OH: Schmul, 1977-1978.
_________. "Quarterly Book-Table." *Methodist Quarterly Review* 38:3 (July 1878) 564-567.

Wiley, H. Orton. *Christian Theology.* 3 vols. Kansas City: Beacon Hill, 1940-1943.

Williams, Henry W. *An Exposition of St. Paul's Epistle to the Romans.* London: Wesleyan Conference Office, 1869.

Williams, William G. *An Exposition of the Epistle of Paul to the Romans.* New York: Eaton & Mains, 1902.

Winchell, Alexander. *Adamites and Pre-Adamites: A Popular Discussion Concerning the Remote Representations of the Human Species and their Relation to the Biblical Adam.* Syracuse, NY: J. T. Roberts, 1878.

For and in-depth contrast between dispensationalism and Wesleyan eschatology, see Vic Reasoner, *The Hope of the Gospel: An Introduction to Wesleyan Eschatology.* Evansville, IN: Fundamental Wesleyan Publishers, 1999.

www.ingramcontent.com/pod-product-compliance
Lightning Source LLC
LaVergne TN
LVHW011052110826
845149LV00015B/3471